The Medieval World

Arts and Literature
in the
Middle Ages

WITHDRAWN **Marc Cels**

 Crabtree Publishing Company
www.crabtreebooks.com

Crabtree Publishing Company

www.crabtreebooks.com

Coordinating editor: Ellen Rodger

Project editor: Carrie Gleason

Designer and production coordinator: Rosie Gowsell

Production assistant: Samara Parent

Scanning technician: Arlene Arch-Wilson

Art director: Rob MacGregor

Project development, editing, photo editing, and layout:
First Folio Resource Group, Inc.: Tom Dart, Debbie Smith,
Anikó Szocs

Proofreading: Lynne Elliott

Photo research: Maria DeCambra

Consultant: Isabelle Cochelin, University of Toronto

Photographs: Alinari/Art Resource, NY: cover, p. 29 (bottom);
Paul Almasy/Corbis/Magma: p. 8 (bottom left); Archivo
Capitular, Tortosa, Spain/Index/Bridgeman Art Library: p. 19
(bottom); Art Archive/Biblioteca Nazionale Marciana
Venice/Dagli Orti: p. 21 (bottom left); Art Archive/British
Library: p. 20, p. 22 (left), p. 24 (right), p. 25 (right); Art
Archive/Dagli Orti: p. 12, p. 15 (bottom right); Art Resource, NY:
p. 13 (left); Bettmann/Corbis/Magma: p. 27 (bottom left);
Biblioteca Marciana, Venice, Italy/Giraudon/Bridgeman Art
Library: p. 24 (left); British Library/Add. 27697 f.197: p. 19 (top);
British Library/Topham-HIP/The Image Works: p. 6, p. 25 (left);
British Museum/Topham-HIP/The Image Works: p. 9 (left);
Cathedral Museum of St. Lazare, Autun, Burgundy,
France/Bridgeman Art Library: p. 8 (top right); Chartreuse de
Champmol, Dijon, France/Lauros/Giraudon/Bridgeman Art
Library: p. 9 (right); Gianni Dagli Orti/Corbis/Magma: p. 21 (top
right), p. 26 (top right); Howard Davie/Private Collection/
Bridgeman Art Library: p. 23 (top); Giraudon/Art Resource, NY:
p. 7 (top), p. 10 (top); The Granger Collection, New York: p. 17
(both), p. 28 (top right); HIP/Scala/Art Resource, NY: p. 16 (left),
p. 18; Erich Lessing/Art Resource, NY: p. 15 (top left), p. 16
(right), p. 29 (top); Mary Evans Picture Library/Evan Wallace
Collection: p. 22 (right); Musée Marmottan, Paris, France/
Giraudon/Bridgeman Art Library: title page; Notre Dame,
Semur-en-Auxois, France/Lauros/Giraudon/Bridgeman Art
Library: p. 10 (bottom); Roger Perrin/Bridgeman Art Library:
p. 23 (bottom); Private Collection/Johnny Van Haeften Ltd.,
London/Bridgeman Art Library: p. 28 (bottom left); Scala/Art
Resource, NY: p. 5 (bottom right), p. 7 (bottom), p. 13 (right),
p. 14 (both)

Map: Samara Parent, Margaret Amy Reiach

Illustrations: Jeff Crosby: p. 11 (all), pp. 30–31; Connie Gleason:
p. 26 (bottom left, bottom right), p. 27 (top and right); Katherine
Kantor: flags, title page (border), copyright page (bottom);
Margaret Amy Reiach: borders, gold boxes, title page (illuminated
letter), copyright page (top), contents page (background), pp. 4-5
(timeline), p. 32 (all)

Cover: This work of art by Italian painter Stefano da Verona
(1375-1438), shows angels singing. Much of the art of the Middle
Ages showed religious figures.

Title page: In the Middle Ages, scribes copied and decorated
books by hand at slanted writing desks.

Crabtree Publishing Company

www.crabtreebooks.com   1-800-387-7650

Cataloging-in-Publication data
Mark Cels
  Arts and literature in the Middle Ages / Mark Cels.
    p. cm. -- (The Medieval World)
  Includes index.
  ISBN 0-7787-1355-5 (RLB) -- ISBN 0-7787-1387-3 (pbk)
    1. Arts, Medieval--Juvenile literature. I. Yitle. II.
Medieval worlds series
NX449.C45 2005
700'.9'02--dc22
                                        2004013101
                                          LC

Published in
the United States
PMB 16A
350 Fifth Ave.
Suite 3308
New York, NY
10118

Published
in Canada
616 Welland Ave.,
St. Catharines,
Ontario, Canada
L2M 5V6

Published in the
United Kingdom
73 Lime Walk
Headington
Oxford
OX3 7AD
United Kingdom

Published
in Australia
386 Mt. Alexander Rd.,
Ascot Vale (Melbourne)
V1C 3032

Table of Contents

The Middle Ages

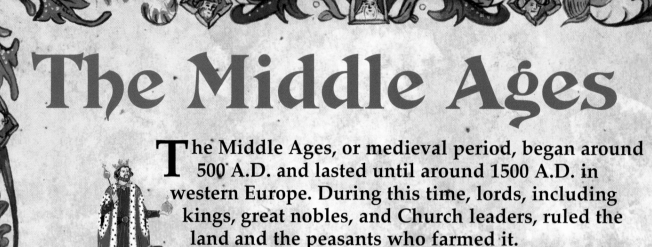

The Middle Ages, or medieval period, began around 500 A.D. and lasted until around 1500 A.D. in western Europe. During this time, lords, including kings, great nobles, and Church leaders, ruled the land and the peasants who farmed it.

Lords hired craftspeople and artists to design and decorate buildings. They paid authors to write about religion and brave warriors, and performers to sing, play music, and tell stories for them. As towns and cities grew, wealthy **merchants** also bought art and books from artists and writers.

Religion and Art

Much of the art, music, and literature from the Middle Ages was about religion. Most Europeans were Christians who believed in one God and followed the teachings of Jesus Christ, who they believed to be God's son. Beautiful churches were built and prayers were sung to honor God. Paintings and carvings decorated the churches and taught people stories from the **Bible**.

▲ *During the Middle Ages, lords controlled almost all the land and wealth, but the population was made up mostly of peasants. Some people lived in towns and became craftspeople who made art for nobles and the Church.*

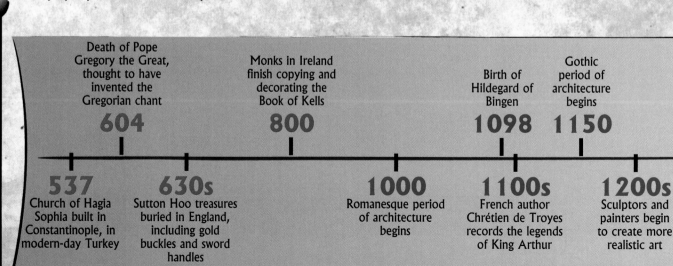

604
Death of Pope Gregory the Great, thought to have invented the Gregorian chant

800
Monks in Ireland finish copying and decorating the Book of Kells

1098
Birth of Hildegard of Bingen

1150
Gothic period of architecture begins

537
Church of Hagia Sophia built in Constantinople, in modern-day Turkey

630s
Sutton Hoo treasures buried in England, including gold buckles and sword handles

1000
Romanesque period of architecture begins

1100s
French author Chrétien de Troyes records the legends of King Arthur

1200s
Sculptors and painters begin to create more realistic art

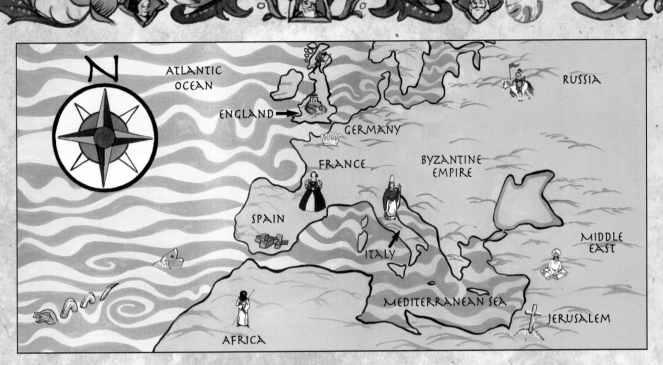

Artists in the Middle Ages

Most medieval artists were men, but women also made crafts. The names of many artists from the Middle Ages are unknown because art was often made by groups of craftspeople who rarely signed their work. They were not considered as important as the patrons, who paid for the art.

▶ *Christians in the Middle Ages believed that giving art to churches pleased God. The husband and wife who paid for this painting by Jan van Eyck (1390–1441) are shown in the bottom corners.*

▲ *By studying the work of medieval painters such as Giotto di Bondone, from Italy, authors such as Geoffrey Chaucer, from England, and composers such as Hildegard of Bingen, from Germany, people today learn what life was like in western Europe long ago.*

Italian painter Giotto di Bondone finishes painting the Arena Chapel in Padua, Italy
1305

English poet Geoffrey Chaucer begins to write The Canterbury Tales
1386

1310
Italian poet Dante Alighieri begins to write The Divine Comedy

1405
Christine de Pisan writes The Book of the City of Ladies in France

Architecture

The most famous buildings from the Middle Ages are castles and cathedrals constructed out of stone. Unlike earlier buildings made of wood, stone buildings did not rot and were less likely to be destroyed by fire.

Castles

Nobles ruled their lands from the safety of their castles, where they lived with their families and **knights**. The castles were built to defend against attacks from invaders. The first medieval castles had a motte and bailey. The motte was a hill on which stood a wooden tower, called a keep, where the noble lived. The bailey was a yard at the bottom of the motte. It was filled with workshops, stables, and barns enclosed by a wooden wall.

In the 1100s, nobles started building stronger castles with thick stone walls. Guards standing on the walls looked out for enemies through slits called merlons. Castles also had towers with narrow windows, called arrowloops, from which **archers** shot at attackers. Some castles were surrounded by moats, or ditches filled with water. People crossed the moats by drawbridges, which could be raised to keep out attackers.

▼ Walls surrounding towns had many of the same defensive features as castle walls, including watchtowers and arrowloops.

Cathedrals

A cathedral was a large stone church that served as the headquarters of the bishop, a church leader who supervised a large area called a diocese. Each bishop had a throne, called a *cathedra*, inside his cathedral.

Cathedrals built from 1000 to 1150 were constructed in the Romanesque style. They had round arches, thick pillars, and thick walls to support their heavy stone ceilings. By 1150, churches were being built in the Gothic style. Gothic cathedrals used tall, thin columns, pointed arches, and **flying buttresses**, instead of thick walls, to support the weight of very high ceilings.

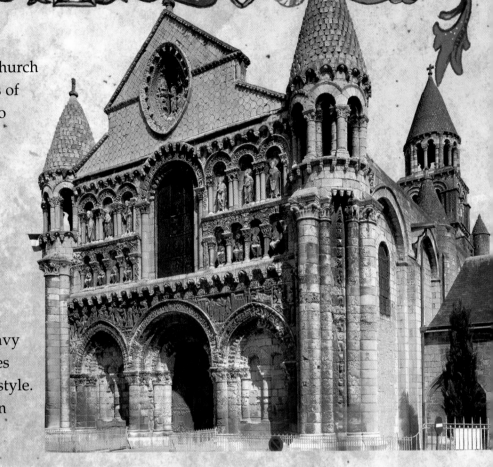

▲ *Towers, carvings, and large doorways decorated this Romanesque cathedral in Poitiers, France.*

Byzantine Architecture

During the Middle Ages, southeastern Europe was ruled by the **Byzantine Empire**, whose **architects** used rounded columns and arches for doorways, ceilings, and windows. Churches, such as this one at the Hosios Loukas **monastery**, in Greece, were often topped with rounded domes. Inside the churches, walls and ceilings were decorated with mosaic pictures formed from thousands of tiny colored tiles.

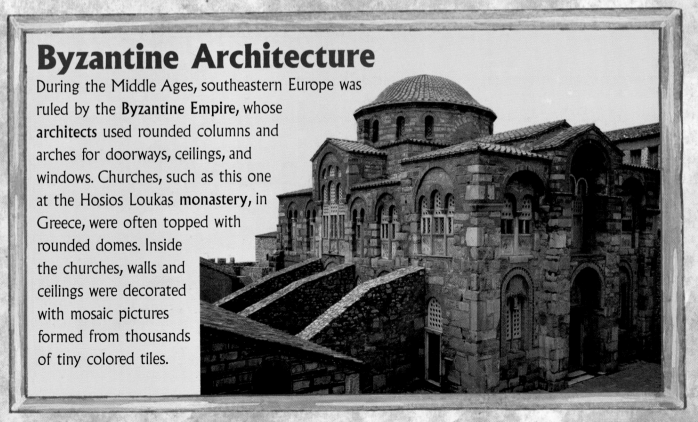

Sculptures

Sculptors used stone, wood, and ivory to decorate furniture and doors in nobles' homes and to make statues and reliefs for churches. Reliefs are figures and designs carved so they are raised from their background.

To make a sculpture, a carver first removed large pieces of stone, wood, or ivory using an ax or a type of ax called an adze, leaving a rough outline of the shape. Next, chisels were used to carve out smaller pieces until the sculpture was nearly done. Finer details were added using smaller chisels, knives, and hand drills. The sculpture was polished, painted, and sometimes decorated with thin sheets of gold.

Large projects, such as making a group of statues for the front of a cathedral, were often divided among craftspeople. Some sculptors carved the bodies, others carved the hair, and still others carved the clothing and faces.

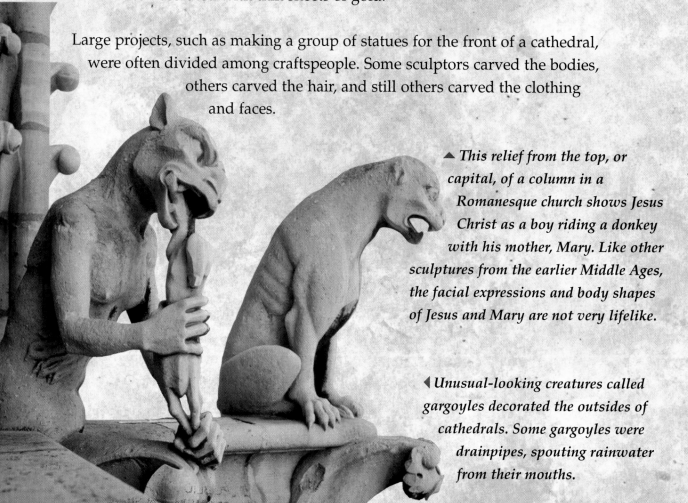

▲ *This relief from the top, or capital, of a column in a Romanesque church shows Jesus Christ as a boy riding a donkey with his mother, Mary. Like other sculptures from the earlier Middle Ages, the facial expressions and body shapes of Jesus and Mary are not very lifelike.*

◀ *Unusual-looking creatures called gargoyles decorated the outsides of cathedrals. Some gargoyles were drainpipes, spouting rainwater from their mouths.*

Late Medieval Sculpture

Early medieval sculptors did not portray people in realistic ways. Only in the later Middle Ages did they create more lifelike work, including portraits of nobles for their palaces and tombs. Sculptors studied the human body and even examined dead bodies to learn the correct positions of bones and muscles.

▶ *The faces, beards, and clothing of these stone statues look very realistic. The statues were carved in the late 1300s for a fountain at a monastery in Champmol, France.*

African Sculpture

Sculptors around the world carved whatever material was available locally. Artists in the medieval kingdoms of West Africa sculpted boxes, heads, and drinking cups from clay, stone, metal, wood, and ivory. These objects were used in ceremonies that honored the spirits of their kings' ancestors.

◀ *Benin, in present-day Nigeria, was one of the wealthiest West African kingdoms between 1000 and 1600. An artist from Benin carved this fine ivory mask and decorated it with pieces of metal.*

Stained-Glass Windows

In the Middle Ages, pictures made of colored, or stained, glass decorated Gothic cathedrals and other large churches. Sunlight passing through the stained glass filled the churches with multicolored light.

Rose Windows

The most spectacular stained-glass windows from the Middle Ages are the large, round rose windows over the doors of Gothic cathedrals. A rose window's delicate web of stone and glass resembles the petals of an open rose or the spokes of a wheel. At the center of each rose window is usually an image of Jesus Christ judging the **souls** of the dead, or his mother Mary surrounded by **saints**. Some rose windows also had pictures showing the months and seasons of the year.

▼ *Beautiful red and blue glass fill this rose window in Chartres Cathedral, in France. It was made in the 1200s and paid for by France's Queen Blanche.*

▶ *Stained-glass windows sometimes show craftspeople and merchants at work, since they often paid to have the windows made. This window shows a craftsperson finishing cloth.*

Making Stained-Glass Windows

Making stained-glass windows required the talents of several craftspeople. Glassmakers made glass, glaziers cut and fit glass into frames to form pictures, and glasspainters painted details on the glass.

▲ ① *Glassmakers made glass by mixing sand, potash, which is made from wood ashes, and metals such as copper, cobalt, and manganese. The metals added color. The mixture was baked in an oven called a kiln until it melted into a liquid.*

▶ ② *Glassmakers used long, metal pipes to blow the hot liquid glass into the shape of a cylinder. Then, they cut the cylinder lengthwise and flattened it into a rectangular sheet.*

◀ ③ *On a wooden table, glaziers drew a full-sized picture of the scene they wanted to make. They laid the colored glass on top of the picture and cut it into the required shapes with a tool called a dividing iron, which had a red-hot point.*

▼ ④ *Glasspainters painted details, such as the folds of cloth and facial features, on the glass. The glass was then placed in a kiln to seal the paint.*

▼ ⑤ *The prepared glass pieces were fitted together with strips of lead and placed in a church's window frame.*

Paintings and Mosaics

Medieval painters painted pictures in books, on wooden panels, and on church walls. For most of the Middle Ages, artists did not paint in a realistic style. Saints or rulers were shown larger than other people to emphasize their importance. They were painted on backgrounds of gold or colorful patterns rather than in natural settings, such as next to hills, trees, or buildings.

The Art of Painting

Paints were made by grinding color pigments, which are powders made from plants and **minerals**, with a little water under a flat stone grinder called a muller. Egg yolk, linseed oil, or walnut oil was added to the ground pigments to thicken it. Paintbrushes were made by tying fine animal hair or fur to wooden sticks. Paints were kept in little pots and mixed on a wooden board, called a palette, which the artist held in his hand.

Becoming a Painter

Learning how to become a painter took a long time. Around the age of twelve, children began their training as apprentices to master, or expert, painters. Apprentices lived and worked with the masters. At first, they did simple tasks, such as cleaning workshops and fetching supplies. Gradually, they were taught more difficult skills, such as drawing, then finally painting.

▲ *Medieval painters usually depicted Jesus and saints with light-filled circles, called halos, around their heads.*

▲ *Apprentices learned how to paint by helping a master with simple jobs, such as grinding pigments and mixing paints.*

Joining the Guild

After working with a master for about six years, an apprentice became a paid craftsperson, called a journeyman, in the workshop of a master painter. The journeyman prepared a special painting, called a masterpiece, and showed it to the guild of painters. Guilds were groups of craftspeople who ensured the quality of their members' work and set prices for their crafts. If the guild judged the work to be good enough, the journeyman became a master painter, was admitted to the guild, and was allowed to set up his own workshop.

Frescoes

In medieval Europe, frescoes decorated churches, palaces, and other buildings. A fresco is a style of painting in which paint is applied to wet plaster walls. This produces bright colors that can be seen from a distance. Fresco artists have to work quickly before the plaster dries. If they want to make changes, they scrape off patches of plaster and start the section again.

Giotto

Giotto di Bondone, who lived from about 1267 to 1337, was an Italian master painter and architect. He was best known for his church frescoes, in which he tried new ways to make paintings more lifelike. Giotto painted figures with the correct body sizes and showed emotions with realistic facial expressions and hand gestures. He also used shadowing to create depth, and he placed his figures in more realistic settings, surrounded by buildings or landscapes.

▲ *The Basilica of Saint Francis in Assisi, Italy, was decorated with frescoes by Giotto di Bondone or his students. This famous fresco shows Saint Francis, who loved animals and nature, preaching the word of God to birds.*

Painted Altarpieces

Altarpieces are religious artworks that decorate the space above and behind a church's **altar**. They are meant to inspire people while they worship. To make an altarpiece in the Middle Ages, an apprentice covered a wooden panel with a mixture of glue and white plaster called gesso. Once the gesso was dry, a master painter drew a rough sketch with charcoal or ink. Then, paint was added over the sketch. Pieces of glass, beads, or thin strips of gold sometimes decorated the altarpiece.

▲ *Medieval altarpieces were often painted on two or more hinged wooden panels that unfolded.*

Icons

Icons are paintings of religious figures. They were made by medieval artists in eastern Europe and the African country of Ethiopia. Most of the artists were **monks** who, rather than creating realistic pictures, showed the figures' religious power by painting eyes and foreheads very large, bodies very long, and faces with serious expressions. Worshipers prayed and lit candles and **incense** in front of the icons. Many believed that the icons held special powers to protect them.

◀ *Icons, such as this Russian icon of the angel Gabriel, often only showed a holy person's head and face.*

Mosaics

Medieval artists made mosaics to decorate floors, walls, and ceilings of churches. Mosaics are pictures created from tiny square tiles of colored glass or stone. The tiles did not fade like paint, and have remained bright for hundreds of years. The most famous mosaics were made by Byzantine artists who created very detailed religious pictures with sparkling backgrounds of golden tiles.

▲ *This mosaic from the church of Hagia Sophia in Constantinople, the capital of the Byzantine Empire, shows Jesus Christ sitting on a throne, with the Empress Zoë and her husband Emperor Constantine IX at his side.*

Muslim Art

In the Middle Ages, craftspeople in Muslim regions, such as southern Spain, North Africa, the **Middle East,** and western Asia, decorated their places of worship, called mosques, with stone carvings and painted tiles. The tiles were covered with geometric patterns, designs of plants, and passages from the *Qur'an*, the Muslim holy book, written in beautiful writing called calligraphy.

▶ *Muslim craftspeople created beautiful and complicated designs with colorful tiles.*

Pottery, Metalwork, and Weavings

Medieval craftspeople were skilled in working with metal, jewels, cloth, and clay. Potters shaped bowls, pots, and jugs from clay as it spun on a potter's wheel. Once the pottery was dry, it was covered with glaze, which formed a glassy surface when baked in a kiln. Adding minerals to the glaze gave it color.

Metalwork

Medieval metalworkers made pots from copper, tin, and bronze, as well as weapons and tools from iron. The finest metals, silver and gold, were worked by skilled craftspeople called goldsmiths. They made buckles, crowns, and jewelry for nobles, as well as crosses, candlesticks, and other items for churches. Designs were often hammered or carved into the metal, and jewels decorated the objects.

▲ *In medieval China, craftspeople made vases, dishes, and statues out of porcelain. Porcelain was made from a special white clay, called kaolin. When baked at high temperatures, it became very hard, smooth, and* translucent.

◀ *This golden belt buckle, with a complicated, intertwining design, was buried in a king's grave in Sutton Hoo, England, around the year 630.*

Tapestries

The stone walls of churches, castles, and wealthy merchants' homes were decorated with tapestries. Tapestries are heavy woven cloth wall hangings. Medieval craftspeople wove tapestries on machines called looms, using threads of wool, linen, silk, and even silver and gold. The tapestries told stories from the Bible or from literature, or showed scenes such as nobles hunting.

▲ *The Lady and the Unicorn is a famous series of six tapestries made in Belgium in the 1480s. The tapestries show a noble lady with an imaginary beast called the unicorn.*

Rugs

Nomadic peoples who lived in central Asia, the area between China and the Middle East, wove rugs to cover the floors of their tents. Muslims kneeled on other rugs, known as prayer rugs, while they worshiped. Each people had its own traditional designs of colorful geometric shapes, animals, plants, and letters. Medieval merchants brought these rugs to western Europe to decorate the walls, floors, and even tables of noble homes and churches.

◀ *Colored wool, cotton, and silk yarns were used to make rugs, such as this one from Persia, which is present-day Iran.*

Beautiful Books

For most of the Middle Ages, books were hand copied by scribes. The books, called manuscripts, took a long time to make, and the materials scribes used were expensive. Only churches, nobles, and wealthy merchants could afford to own books.

At first, most scribes were monks or **nuns** who worked in monasteries copying religious books, such as the Bible. After 1200 A.D., craftspeople in towns also worked as scribes, copying books about history, science, medicine, and law.

Parchment to Paper

Scribes wrote with pens made from goose feathers called quills. The sharpened end of the quill was dipped in ink made from water and soot, and thickened with tree sap. Most manuscripts were copied on sheets of thin, cleaned sheepskin or calfskin, called parchment. The animal hides were soaked for days in water and **lye** to soften them and remove the hair and grease. After being rinsed in clean water, the hides were stretched on wooden frames, scraped smooth, and dried out.

In the later Middle Ages, scribes began writing on paper. Paper was invented in China around 100 A.D., but it was not well known in Europe before the 1200s. Paper was easier and less expensive to make than parchment. Pulp was made by shredding old linen rags in water. The pulp was scooped up in a square frame that had a wire mesh bottom through which the water drained. The thin sheet of pulp left behind was pressed and dried to form a sheet of paper.

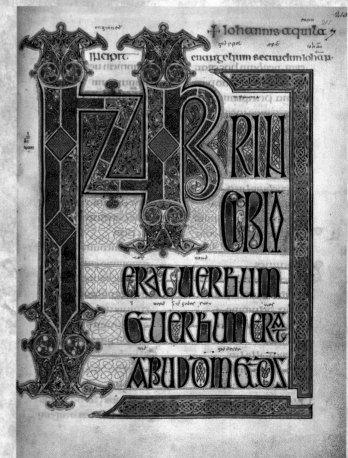

▼ *From the 600s to the 900s, monks from Ireland and Britain made Bibles with very complicated, colorful, finely painted patterns. This page from the Lindisfarne Gospels has large initial letters decorated with spirals, knots, and tiny dots.*

Decorating a Manuscript

Scribes and artists called illuminators decorated some manuscripts with vibrantly colored inks, paints, and thin sheets of gold. Large initial letters and borders were filled with small painted pictures called miniatures. These manuscripts were called illuminated manuscripts because their pages seemed to be illuminated or glowing with light. The covers of expensive Bibles were also decorated with panels of gold, silver, or ivory.

▶ *Beautifully decorated prayer books called Books of Hours were made for nobles. This page from a Book of Hours shows saints and angels in Heaven. The bright blue paint was made by grinding a rare and expensive stone from central Asia called lapis lazuli.*

▼ *A picture of a jester decorates an initial letter in this book of prayers. A jester was a clown who sang and danced for nobles.*

Literature

Most medieval books were written in Latin, the language used by the Church and educated people. There were Latin books of poetry, myths, history, science, and philosophy, as well as books about religion.

Europeans in the Middle Ages also created stories, poems, and songs in their everyday languages. At first, these stories were told aloud, but by the 1100s, they were being written down. Many of these stories are still popular today.

Storytellers

Stories were told as people sat around the fire at night, rested from work, or traveled. Minstrels, or jongleurs, were paid to sing, dance, juggle, joke, act, play music, and tell stories in the homes of nobles, as well as in village and town markets. Harp-poets, or troubadours, were hired by nobles to compose and sing poems about their victories in war and the deeds of their ancestors.

Epics

Epics were long poems sung aloud that described the lives and battles of brave warriors. *Beowulf* is an English epic that tells of the young warrior Beowulf. Beowulf earns fame and riches by killing a man-eating swamp monster named Grendel and Grendel's vengeful mother. Fifty years later, Beowulf fights again, this time against a flying, fire-breathing dragon. Beowulf kills the dragon, but is also killed himself.

▲ The story of *Beowulf* was first told in the 700s, but it was not written down until after 1000. This is the first page from the only manuscript of *Beowulf* that has survived from the Middle Ages.

Roland and El Cid

La Chanson de Roland, or *The Song of Roland,* is a French epic from the 1000s that tells of a brave warrior named Roland. Roland served his uncle, the Christian emperor Charlemagne, during his war with Spain in 778. In the story, Roland is **betrayed** by one of his fellow warriors and is attacked on his march back to France. Charlemagne hears the sound of Roland's horn calling for help, but he arrives to find that Roland and his men have died in battle. The poem ends with the trial and execution, or putting to death, of the warrior who betrayed Roland.

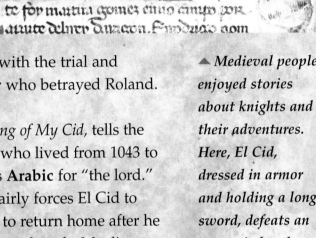

▲ *Medieval people enjoyed stories about knights and their adventures. Here, El Cid, dressed in armor and holding a long sword, defeats an enemy in battle.*

The Spanish epic *Cantar de Mío Cid,* or *The Song of My Cid,* tells the story of a real Spanish knight, Rodrigo Díaz, who lived from 1043 to 1099. Díaz was nicknamed "El Cid," which is **Arabic** for "the lord." The epic describes how the Spanish king unfairly forces El Cid to leave his homeland. El Cid is finally allowed to return home after he and his knights win a great victory against the ruler of a Muslim kingdom in Spain.

◄ *Knights who heard the Song of Roland hoped to be as brave in the face of death as Roland had been. This illustration shows an angel dressed as a knight coming to lead Roland's soul to Heaven.*

Viking Sagas

The Vikings of northern Europe were traders and fierce warriors who attacked settlements throughout Europe from the 700s to the 900s. Their stories, or sagas, tell about their adventures, battles, loves, and families. The sagas were passed along orally and written down in the 1200s by storytellers in Iceland. One of the most famous sagas is *Erik the Red's Saga*, which tells about the adventures of Erik the Red, a Viking who sailed to Greenland after being banished from Iceland for committing a murder.

▶ *Erik the Red founded two Viking communities in Greenland that lasted until about 1400.*

▲ *As the dreamer in the* **Romance of the Rose** *searches for his true love, he meets many characters who represent different stages of falling in love.*

Tales of Chivalry and Romance

Romances were long poems and stories that told about the battles and loves of ancient warriors and taught lessons about **chivalry**. They were written by troubadours for nobles in France.

The *Romance of the Rose* is a long poem begun by the French author Guillaume de Lorris around 1237 and finished by Jean de Meun in 1280. It describes a dream in which the dreamer searches for his true love, the Rose, in a walled garden.

Some of the most popular heroes of medieval romances were members of the court of the legendary King Arthur. Arthur was the son of a king who grew up not knowing about his royal blood. One day, it was announced that the next king would be the man who could pull a sword, named Excalibur, out of a stone where it had been stuck for years. Arthur succeeded and became king. The romances tell of the adventures of Arthur, his queen, Guinevere, the wizard Merlin, and Arthur's knights, including Lancelot, Gawain, and Perceval.

Robin Hood

The *Gest of Robin Hood* was one of several songs by English minstrels. Robin Hood is a legendary archer who led a group of **outlaws** known as his merry men. They lived in a forest, where they robbed travelers. Later storytellers made up more adventures about Robin and added characters such as Little John, Will Scarlet, and Much the Miller's Son. They also made Robin and his merry men into heroes who stole from the rich to give to the poor.

Short Stories

Medieval people enjoyed listening to short stories and poems. Some stories told about the miracles of saints and inspired listeners' religious beliefs. Others were fables. Fables often have animal characters and teach **moral** lessons, such as the dangers of being jealous, greedy, or lazy. Fabliaux were humorous short poems written in the 1100s and 1300s. They usually told about clever heroes or heroines who tricked their way through adventures. Instead of practicing chivalrous manners, characters in fabliaux often lied, swore, and cheated.

▲ *Robin Hood continues to be a popular character in books and films. This modern illustration shows him competing in an archery contest near the castle of Nottingham, in England.*

The Thousand and One Nights

The Thousand and One Nights is a collection of Arab, **Persian**, and Indian stories gathered in Iraq in the 900s. The tales are woven together by the fictional character Scheherazade, who tells a story every night to entertain her cruel husband, King Sharyar. Sharyar has had each of his previous brides killed the morning after their wedding to prevent them from being unfaithful. Scheherazade tells her stories for 1,001 nights, long enough to prove her faithfulness and soften the king's heart. The tales include the stories of "Aladdin," "Ali Baba and the Forty Thieves," and "Sinbad the Sailor."

▲ *Sinbad and his crew set sail on many journeys to seek treasures and battle enemies.*

Famous Writers

While the authors of many medieval books are unknown, some, such as Dante Alighieri and Geoffrey Chaucer, became famous and their books are still studied today. Their literature describes the lives, thoughts, and feelings of people in the Middle Ages.

Li Po ▶

Li Po (701–762) was a famous Chinese poet. He spent most of his life traveling through China, writing about the country's beautiful landscape, his friends, and his love of wine. For a short time, he wrote poetry for the Chinese emperor's son, but was sent away after the son was executed for trying to establish his own kingdom. Li Po was eventually pardoned, or forgiven, and died in a relative's home, although legend says that he drowned falling out of a boat while trying to grab the reflection of the moon on the water.

◀ Dante Alighieri

Dante Alighieri (1265–1321) was an Italian poet and politician, who also had a great knowledge of religion, science, and history. His most famous work is a very long poem called *The Divine Comedy*. The poem tells of Dante's imaginary journey through the Christian **afterlife** to meet the souls of famous dead people. He first visits the deep pit of Hell, where he meets the souls of sinners who are punished for their crimes. Then, he goes to the Mountain of **Purgatory**, where he meets souls climbing up to Heaven. Finally, in Heaven, or Paradise, he speaks with saints who lead him to God.

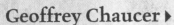

Geoffrey Chaucer ▶

Geoffrey Chaucer lived from about 1342 to 1400. This English poet is most famous for his collection of rhyming short stories called the *Canterbury Tales*. The stories are about a group of 29 travelers — including knights, merchants, cooks, and nuns — who go on a religious trip, or pilgrimage, to Canterbury Cathedral in England. Along the way, they take turns telling romances, fables, fabliaux, religious stories, and other tales to entertain one another.

Omar Khayyam

Omar Khayyam (1048–1131) was a Muslim mathematician and poet from Persia. His most famous work is a collection of poems written in Persian called the *Rubáiyát*. The word *ruba'i* refers to a four-line verse in which the first, second, and fourth lines rhyme. In his poems, Khayyam discusses the pleasures of life, **destiny**, and morality.

▼ Christine de Pisan

Christine de Pisan was born in Italy in 1364, but she lived in France for most of her life. She was educated by her father, an **astrologer** in the court of Charles V, King of France. She began to write about love, religion, morality, history, and her own life to support herself and her three children after her husband died. One of her most famous books was *The Book of the City of Ladies*, in which she wrote about great women in history.

Music and Dance

There were two main types of music in the Middle Ages. Religious music was sung and played during worship. Non-religious music included singing and dancing for entertainment.

Musical Instruments

Peasants in the Middle Ages played simple homemade instruments, including pipes made from **reeds**, bones, animal horns, or wood, and drums made from wood and animal skins. Nobles and wealthier townspeople played more complicated instruments, such as harps, which they bought from craftspeople.

▲ Troubadours often sang their poems and stories while playing instruments such as this stringed instrument called a viol.

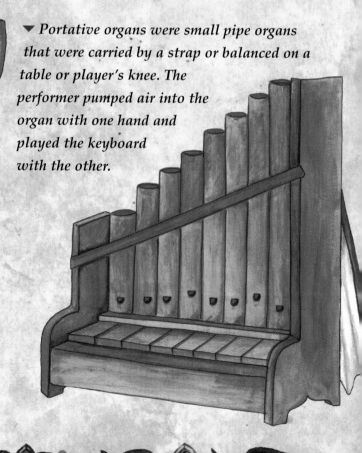

▼ Portative organs were small pipe organs that were carried by a strap or balanced on a table or player's knee. The performer pumped air into the organ with one hand and played the keyboard with the other.

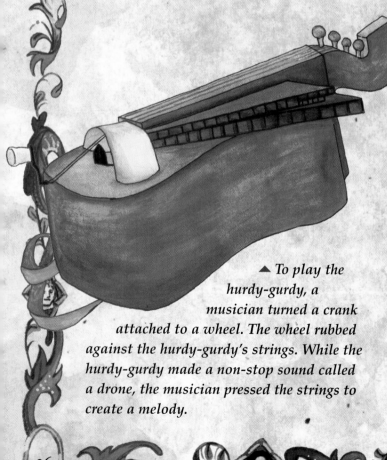

▲ To play the hurdy-gurdy, a musician turned a crank attached to a wheel. The wheel rubbed against the hurdy-gurdy's strings. While the hurdy-gurdy made a non-stop sound called a drone, the musician pressed the strings to create a melody.

From the Middle East and Asia

By 1200, Europeans were playing instruments that had come from the Middle East and Asia. Lutes were pear-shaped stringed instruments similar to Arab instruments called *ouds*. They were played by plucking strings with a feather. Nakers were a pair of small, curved drums hung on a belt. They were similar to Arab drums called *naqqara*.

▶ *Shawms, which resembled oboes, were instruments from Asia that made continuous loud, piercing sounds. A shawm player had to be able to breathe in with the nose and blow out of the mouth at the same time.*

▶ *Long trumpets were first used in the Middle East to signal soldiers during battle. In Europe, they were also used to announce important people.*

Religious Music

The first religious music was called plainsong. Choirs sang chants, based on passages from the Bible, that used the same notes and were not accompanied instruments. The best known type of plainsong was the Gregorian chant.

In the 1100s, instruments were added to religious music. Toward the end of the Middle Ages, composers were paid to write complicated songs in which different voices sang different notes and words at the same time.

◀ *According to legend, Pope Gregory I, who lived from around 540 to 604, was taught what notes to chant by God. God came to him in the form of a dove that spoke in his ear.*

Musical Notation

Medieval people invented different ways to write down notes for religious music. Some wrote symbols above the words in prayer books. Later, scribes drew symbols on red lines. This was the beginning of modern musical notation. Since books were expensive to make, music was often written very large so that a choir could share the same book and read it from a distance.

▲ *Notes for music were written with square and diamond-shaped symbols on lines above the words.*

Music for Special Occasions

Peasants in the countryside celebrated special occasions, such as weddings and festivals, by performing folk songs and dancing to pipes and drums. Townspeople listened to the music and songs of minstrels at fairs, or hired them to play in their homes. Nobles also had musicians perform in their homes at feasts and other special occasions. Guests sometimes took turns singing for each other. By the later Middle Ages, sounds of trumpets could be heard throughout the feast, announcing the beginning of the meal and the start of each course.

◀ *By the later Middle Ages, learning to play instruments, such as lutes, was part of noble children's education.*

Dancing

Medieval people danced at social gatherings, such as celebrations for holy days, wedding parties, and fairs. They danced outdoors or inside halls, but it was considered improper to dance in churches or church yards.

Dancers usually moved in lines or circles as musicians played lively tunes on pipes and drums. On holy days, they danced carols, which were fast circle dances performed around a singing leader. The dancers stopped only to sing the **refrain** of the carol song, which usually told a religious story.

Noble Dances

In the 1300s, nobles invented a formal dance style, called the *basse danse*, that was different from the dance of peasants. In the *basse danse*, groups of couples began by making a bow, called the *révérence*, then they performed a combination of five complicated movements. For example, the *branle* movement involved turning the body left, right, left, right, while keeping the heels together and not moving the feet. Nobles hired dancing instructors to teach their children the proper movements so they could dance at banquets.

▲ *A harp accompanies nobles performing a circle dance outdoors.*

◀ *Nobles dance as a band of minstrels play instruments, including shawms.*

Mystery Plays

Mystery plays were series of short plays performed in towns on holy days. Each play told a Bible story or taught a Christian moral lesson.

The word "mystery" comes from the medieval word *maisterie*, meaning "craft." A different guild of craftworkers paid for each play's costumes and main actors. Guild members performed the smaller roles. Since there were no theaters in the Middle Ages, mystery plays were performed outdoors on decorated wagons. A full series of mystery plays could take all day to perform. The audience participated by cheering the actors who played the heroes and booing the actors who played devils and other villains.

Wagons were pulled around to stations in the town where spectators watched the plays.

The craft guilds that staged each play owned the expensive costumes that the actors wore.

Men and boys acted all the parts, even performing the roles of female characters.

The actors spoke their lines in rhymes.

This play tells the Christmas story about the birth of Jesus Christ.

Performers acted both on and around the wagon stage.

31

Glossary

afterlife Life after death

altar A table or stand used for religious ceremonies

ancestor The person from whom an individual or group of people comes from

Arabic One of the main languages of the Middle East

archer A soldier who shoots an arrow from a bow

architect A person who designs buildings

astrologer A person who studies how the stars, moons, and planets affect events on Earth and human behavior

betray To turn a person over to the enemy

Bible The book of sacred writings believed by Christians to have come from God

Byzantium Empire The area between Europe and Asia, including present day Turkey and Greece, under the rule of Christain emperors from 330 A.D. to 1453 A.D.

chivalry A code of conduct that required knights to be brave and kind

destiny A series of events that have been determined in advance

flying buttress An arched beam that extends outside a building to support its walls

incense A mix of spices that produces a pleasant odor when burned

ivory The hard white material from the tusks of mammals, such as elephants

knight A medieval soldier who fought on horseback

lye A liquid made from wood ashes that is used to wash and make soap

merchant A person who buys and sells goods

Middle East The region made up of southwestern Asia and northern Africa

mineral A substance obtained through mining

monastery A place where religious men or women live, work, and pray

monk A religious man who lives in a monastery and devotes his life to prayer and work

moral Relating to the idea of what is right and wrong

Muslim Belonging to Islam, a religion based on the teachings of God, called Allah, and his prophet Muhammad

nomadic Having no fixed home and moving from place to place in search of food and water

nun A religious woman who lives in a monastery and devotes her life to prayer and work

outlaw A criminal

Persian The language of the people of Iran

philosophy The study of truth, right and wrong, God, and the meaning of life

Purgatory A place where Roman Catholics believe souls go after death to be cleansed of their sins before going to Heaven

reed The hollow stem of a tall grass

refrain The part of a song that is repeated many times

saint A holy person

soul The spiritual part of a human that some people think lives on after death

translucent Clear enough to let light pass through

Index

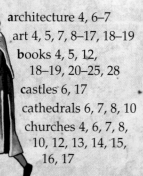

1 2 3 4 5 6 7 8 9 0 Printed in the U.S.A. 1 0 9 8 7 6 5 4